Which two of these animals are the closest relatives?

Hippo

Dolphin

Shark

Two have rubbery fins and ocean homes.
They seem like close cousins—but they're not!
How can that be?

The answer starts with the smallest creature
the world has ever known and ends with the biggest.

It's a story from out of the blue.

For James, with an ocean of love
ES

For the very lovely little Ada
FPG

First edition 2021. Library of Congress Catalog Card Number pending. ISBN 978-1-5362-1410-9. This book was typeset in Memphis. The illustrations were created digitally. Candlewick Press, 99 Dover Street, Somerville, Massachusetts 02144. www.candlewick.com. Printed in Dongguan, Guangdong, China. 21 22 23 24 25 26 TLF 10 9 8 7 6 5 4 3 2 1

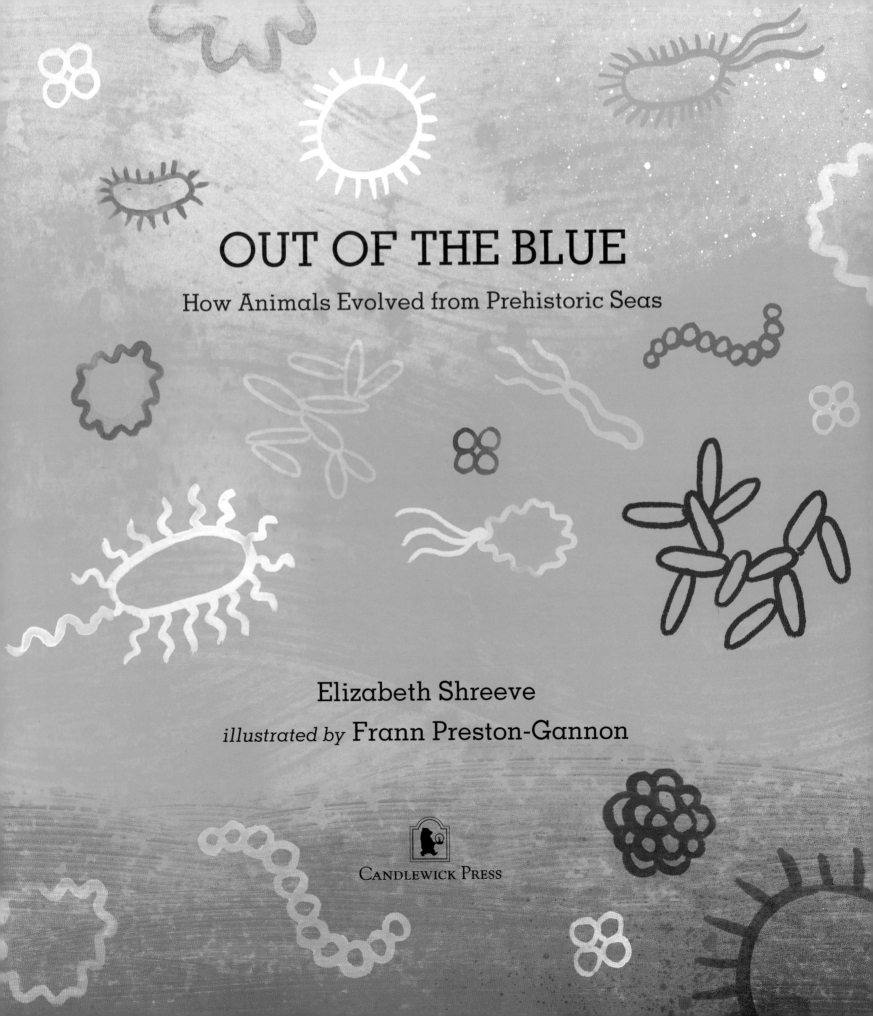

OUT OF THE BLUE

How Animals Evolved from Prehistoric Seas

Elizabeth Shreeve

illustrated by Frann Preston-Gannon

CANDLEWICK PRESS

ARCHEAN EON (4 to 2.5 billion years ago)

LIFE BEGAN in the vast empty sea, when Earth was young.
First came single-celled microbes, much too small to see. Each held
the promise of all life-forms to come.

For billions of years, the microbes thrived in a world that would be
alien to you and me. The sky glowed orange. Fiery volcanoes spewed
poisonous smoke. Sometimes, enormous ice sheets turned our planet
into a gigantic snowball.

In the restless seas, the microbes slowly, slowly changed. They
became more complex. They began to convert sunlight into energy
and produce oxygen. Until finally, at last . . .

Gulp!

One microbe swallowed another.

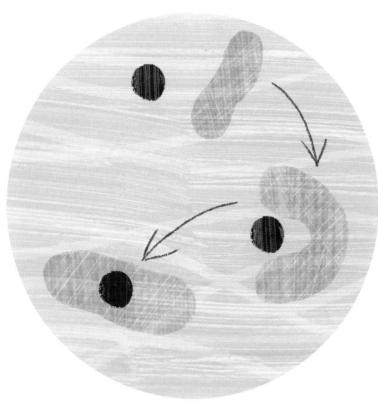

Strange, squishy creatures evolved. They began to hunt. The race was on—eat or be eaten! And that was only the beginning. Because next came . . .

EDIACARAN PERIOD (635 to 541 mya)
mya = million years ago

Jellyfish shaped
like pizzas

Charnia waving
like ferns

Sponges growing in
clumps and tubes

the Cambrian Explosion!

Higher oxygen levels provided fuel for life—
and all the major types of animals began to take shape.

*Mollusks with squishy bodies,
often wrapped in shells*

*Arthropods with tough outer skeletons
and jointed legs (trilobites rule the seas!)*

CAMBRIAN PERIOD (541 to 485 mya)

Chordates, the first creatures with signs of spinal cords, like ours

Annelid worms with segmented bodies

Echinoderms like sea stars and sea urchins

Cnidarians, like sea anemones, armed with stinging cells (beware!)

Predators jetted through the seas, hungry and hunting. Their prey evolved to defend themselves: Prickles! Spines! Armored shells! While above the tide line . . .

CAMBRIAN PERIOD (541 to 485 mya) – **ORDOVICIAN PERIOD** (485 to 444 mya)

land lay bare. Sun's lethal rays beat down.
Nothing could survive.

Wait—what's that? An early pioneer! One of the arthropods—a
tiny millipede—comes onto the land.

Perhaps it floats ashore on a mat of algae or is stranded by the
tide. Five hundred million years later, we find the fossilized trace
of its feet scurrying up the shore. On land it is safe from predators.
But how will it breathe? What will it eat?

SILURIAN PERIOD (444 to 419 mya)

More millipedes and centipedes invade the land. They feed on small worms and plants at the water's edge, and they breathe through holes on the sides of their bodies. Low, mossy plants begin to spread into miniature, millipede-sized jungles.

Scorpions scuttle onshore. Like all arthropods, their hard outer skeletons protect them like armor. These creatures later evolve into our modern-day scorpions, spiders, ticks, and mites.

Back in the ocean, their cousins give rise to sea spiders and huge "sea scorpions" called eurypterids as well as the horseshoe crab, an ancient type of animal that still lives along some shorelines today.

sea scorpion

Life gets busy at the water's edge. And another type of arthropod crawls from the waves—**the crustaceans.**

These shrimp-like animals later evolve into land animals like giant coconut crabs and tiny pill bugs. Their marine cousins eventually become our modern crabs, lobsters, and shrimp.

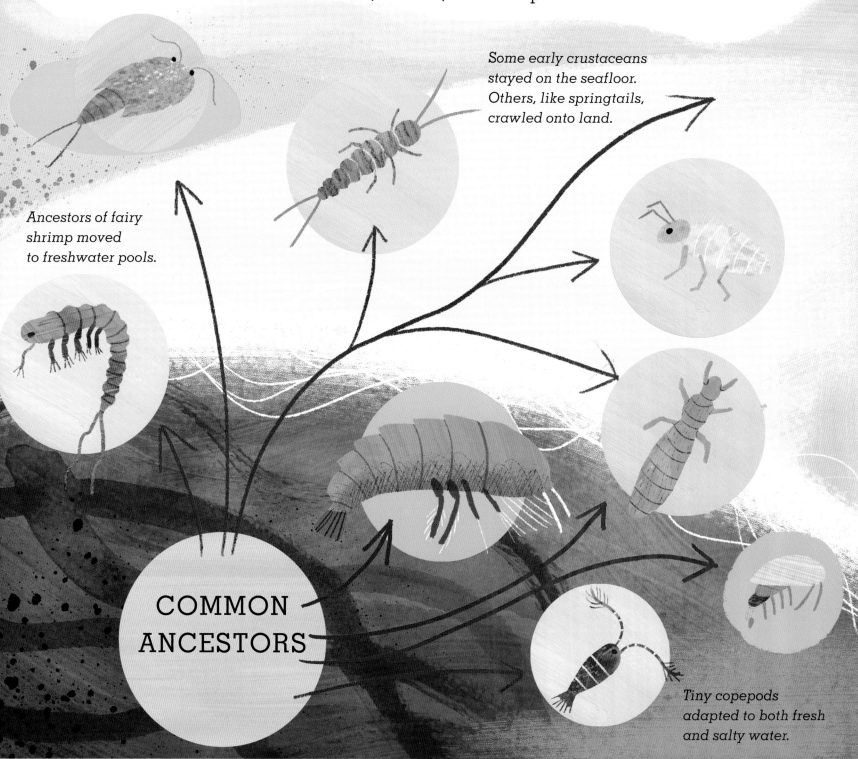

Some early crustaceans stayed on the seafloor. Others, like springtails, crawled onto land.

Ancestors of fairy shrimp moved to freshwater pools.

COMMON ANCESTORS

Tiny copepods adapted to both fresh and salty water.

And here come the insects!

These little arthropods become the first creatures on
Earth to take flight. Millions of years later, when
oxygen levels soar, they grow huge.
Watch out for that dragonfly!

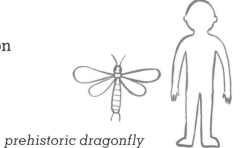

prehistoric dragonfly

DEVONIAN PERIOD (419 to 359 mya) – **CARBONIFEROUS PERIOD** (359 to 299 mya)

A different type of animal squirms onto shore—the mollusks. Some of them evolve into land snails and slugs. Most mollusks stay in the ocean, where they later give rise to modern sea creatures like multi-armed octopuses and squid.

Ancestor of today's clams, octopuses, and squid

DEVONIAN PERIOD (419 to 359 mya) – **CARBONIFEROUS PERIOD** (359 to 299 mya)

But who are all those other creatures
darting through the water?

Land snails developed
lungs to breathe air.

Eight-legged octopuses evolved
around 100 million years ago.

Nautiloids with many different
types of shells

Sea snails that filtered
food from the water

Welcome to the Age of Fishes!

Fish are chordate animals, which means they have spinal cords. This helps them swim fast! Around 400 million years ago, they evolved into a rainbow of colors, sizes, and shapes.

Bony fishes like the lobe-fins and ray-fins

Jawless fishes, like the lampreys and hagfish of today

DEVONIAN PERIOD (419 to 359 mya)

Placoderms like the twenty-foot-long Dunkleosteus,
with heavy armor and bony jaws

Sharks and other cartilaginous fish, with
skeletons of cartilage instead of bone

The ancient seas are filling with fierce predators.
The climate is changing, too. There is less oxygen
in the oceans and more in the air.

What's a poor fish to do?

Helicoprion, a shark-like fish
that evolved later in prehistory

In order to survive, some fish grow bigger.
Some get harder to catch. Others move to
new territories in rivers and streams. The land is
green with mosses, horsetails, and fern-like trees.
Small animals scurry among the plants. There is plenty of food.

Using their strong limbs, lobe-finned fish wiggle onto muddy
banks . . . and begin to gulp air.

DEVONIAN PERIOD (419 to 359 mya) – **CARBONIFEROUS PERIOD** (359 to 299 mya)

Their descendants become four-legged tetrapods, ancestors of all vertebrate animals on land—including people!

Our bodies show the fish inside us.

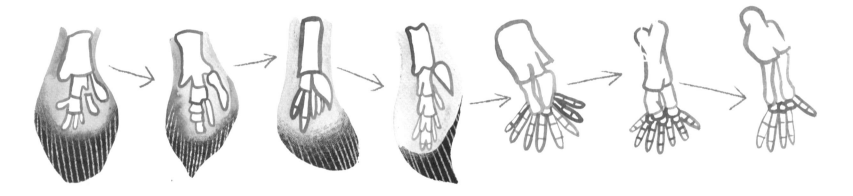

Their fins became our four limbs. Our teeth evolved from their scales. Where they have swim bladders, we have lungs.

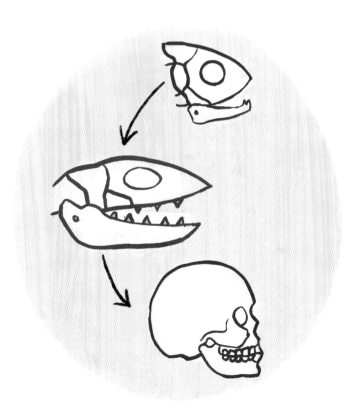

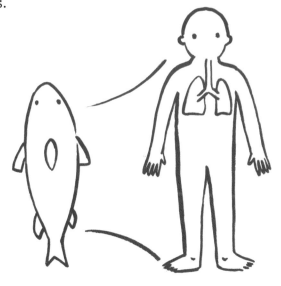

Their gills evolved into our jaws, ears, and throats.

(And one more thing.
Fish get the hiccups, too!)

Long before dinosaurs, animals like Edaphosaurus and Dimetrodon developed sail-like spines.

CARBONIFEROUS PERIOD (359 to 299 mya) – **PERMIAN PERIOD** (299 to 252 mya)

As forests spread, tetrapods evolve into amphibians and reptiles.
Some lay eggs with tough, watertight coverings.
These eggs are important because everything is about to change.
Scientists aren't sure why. They call this event . . .

Some tetrapods became plant-eaters while others, like Eryops, were fierce predators.

Full-grown Seymouria lived on land, but their young lived in water.

the Great Dying.

At the end of the Permian Period, 252 million years ago,

temperatures soar.

Ocean waters grow toxic.

It's the worst extinction in Earth's history.

Almost all types of ocean animals disappear.

Most land animals die off, too.

PERMIAN EXTINCTION (252 mya)

But then, Earth comes alive again—and the balance shifts. Now land supports a wider variety of animals than the oceans. Dinosaurs roam. Pterosaurs take to the skies. Giant reptiles return to the sea as predators.

Hey, look at the furry little creature on that log! It's an early mammal, with sharp hearing and an underground home. Those cozy burrows protect some mammals during the next great extinction . . .

JURASSIC PERIOD (201 to 145 mya)

around 66 million years ago, when an asteroid hits Earth and wipes out all large animals. Dinosaurs disappear, except for birds. Flying pterosaurs are gone, along with big reptiles in the seas.

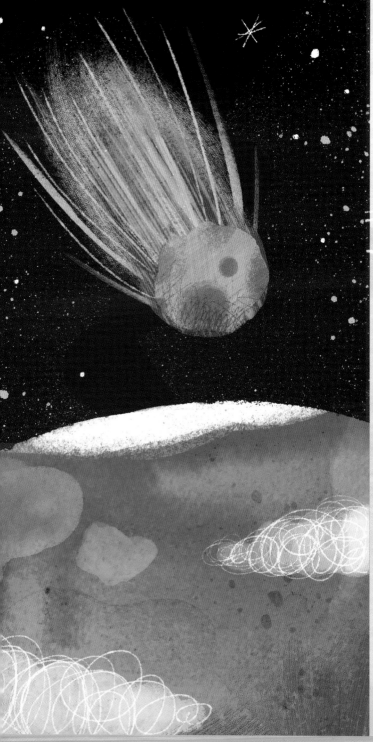

The Age of Mammals begins!

Many types of mammals emerge. They have spinal cords—like those first fish that moved onto land!—and they feed their young with milk. One mammal group develops into large, hoofed animals, like goats and cows.

That group splits . . .

and splits again . . .

and again . . .

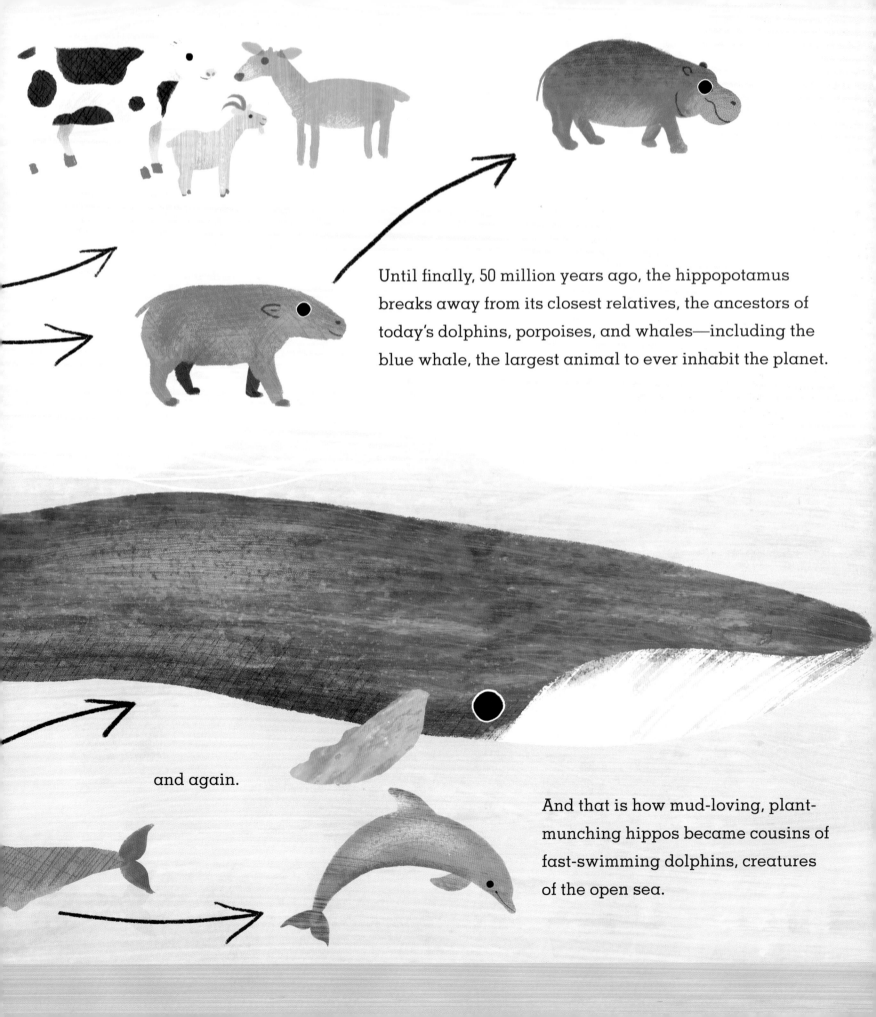

Until finally, 50 million years ago, the hippopotamus breaks away from its closest relatives, the ancestors of today's dolphins, porpoises, and whales—including the blue whale, the largest animal to ever inhabit the planet.

and again.

And that is how mud-loving, plant-munching hippos became cousins of fast-swimming dolphins, creatures of the open sea.

Floating, swimming, wiggling, or walking—
life moves between water and land.
Always changing. Always evolving.

From out of the blue . . .
and back again.

PALEOZOIC ERA (542 to 252 mya)

MESOZOIC ERA (252 to 66 mya)   **CENOZOIC ERA** (66 mya to present)

SELECTED SOURCES

This book led me deep into research on long-ago oceans, those strange and wonderful places that we can barely imagine today. Here are a few of the resources I consulted; please visit my author website for more. https://elizabethshreeve.com/

Marshall, Michael. "Timeline: The Evolution of Life." *New Scientist*, July 14, 2009.

_____. "In the Beginning: The Full Story of Life on Earth Can Finally Be Told." *New Scientist*, January 9, 2019.

Quammen, David. "First There Were Microbes. Then Life on Earth Got Big." *National Geographic*, March 2018.

Shear, William A., and Paul A. Selden. "Rustling in the Undergrowth: Animals in Early Terrestrial Ecosystems." In *Plants Invade the Land: Evolutionary and Environmental Perspectives*, edited by Patricia G. Gensel and Dianne Edwards, 29–51. New York: Columbia University Press, 2001.

Shubin, Neil. *Your Inner Fish: A Journey into the 3.5-Billion-Year History of the Human Body.* New York: Vintage, 2009.

Zimmer, Carl. *At the Water's Edge: Fish with Fingers, Whales with Legs, and How Life Came Ashore but Then Went Back to Sea.* New York: Touchstone, 1998.

Especially for Youngsters

Dixon, Dougal. *When the Whales Walked and Other Incredible Evolutionary Journeys.* London: Quarto Publishing, 2018.

Eons. Season 1, episode 20, "The Search for the Earliest Life." Released February 15, 2018, on PBS Digital Studios. https://www.pbs.org/show/eons/collections/early-life-earth/.

Jenkins, Martin. *Life: The First Four Billion Years.* Somerville, MA: Candlewick Studio, 2019.

Smithsonian Institution. "The Ocean Throughout Geologic Time." https://ocean.si.edu/through-time/ancient-seas/ocean-throughout-geologic-time-image-gallery.

Williams, Martin, dir. *First Life with David Attenborough.* Two-part documentary. Aired October 24, 2010, on Discovery Channel.

Zommer, Yuval. *The Big Book of the Blue.* London: Thames & Hudson, 2018.

ACKNOWLEDGMENTS

I am deeply grateful to the brilliant scientists who reviewed many drafts of this book. Heartfelt thanks to friends at California Academy of Sciences: Jack Dumbacher, John McCosker, and the amazing Rich Mooi. Much appreciation to Will Ratcliff at Georgia Tech and Petra Sierwald at the Field Museum, and special thanks to two experts on early land animals—Paul Selden at the University of Kansas and William Shear at Hampden-Sydney College. Without their help I could never have found my way from oceans of information onto the dry land of a final draft.

Many thanks to Kirsten Hall, who came up with the idea of a book called *Out of the Blue*, and to Frann Preston-Gannon for such gorgeous artwork. Thanks also to my fabulous agent, Ammi-Joan Paquette, and to Katie Cunningham, Alex Robertson, and the crew at Candlewick for undertaking the squiggling, squirming history of animals. Big hugs to writing pals, especially Alexandria Giardino, Darcey Rosenblatt, Lisa Schulman, and my brother, Jamie Shreeve. And loving thanks to Ken and our kids, who always keep me afloat.